D0010037

BLACK AMERICAN FICTION SINCE 1952;

A PRELIMINARY CHECKLIST

by

Frank Deodene and William P. French

THE CHATHAM BOOKSELLER
Chatham, New Jersey

1970

L. C. catalog card number: 78-96384

PREFACE

In this list the compilers have tried to include all first editions of books of fiction by black authors born or living in the United States, published from 1953 to mid-1969, excluding translations (except of works unpublished in English), juveniles and anthologies. Works published before 1953 are listed in Maxwell Whiteman's *A Century of Fiction by American Negroes, 1853-1952* (Philadelphia 1955, reprinted 1968) and Robert A. Bone's *The Negro Novel in America* (Rev. ed., New Haven 1965). For the period since then the best guides have been Janheinz Jahn's *A Bibliography of Neo-African Literature* (New York 1965), and Arthur B. Spingarn's annual listing "Books by Negro Authors" (now discontinued) in the NAACP magazine *Crisis*.

The first novel by a black American, William Wells Brown's *Clotel*, was published in 1853, a year after *Uncle Tom's Cabin*. In 1952 Ralph Ellison's *Invisible Man* marked the black novel's first century. In the eighteen years since, many more works have appeared than in the preceding century, and, while the range of subject-matter and approach has increased correspondingly, so has the cohesiveness and distinction of black fiction generally.

The compilers will be grateful for any additions and corrections, which may be sent to the addresses below.

Frank Deodene	William P. French
The Chatham Bookseller	University Place Book Shop
38 Maple Street	840 Broadway
Chatham, N. J. 07928	New York, N.Y. 10003

Anderson, Alston. All God's Children. Indianapolis, Bobbs, 1965. 221p. *A novel about the life and character of October Pruitt, a slave born in Virginia in 1824.*

Anderson, Alston. Lover Man. N.Y., Doubleday, 1959. 177p. *A collection of short stories about American blacks, by a young West Indian, educated at a black college in North Carolina.*

Anderson, Henry L. No Use Cryin'. London & Los Angeles, Western Publishers, 1961. 208p.

Austin, Edmund O. The Black Challenge. N.Y., Vantage, 1958. 230p. *Novel based on the Garvey movement. Author born in West Indies.*

Baldwin, James. Another Country. N.Y., Dial, 1962. 436p.

Baldwin, James. Giovanni's Room. N.Y., Dial, 1956. 248p.

Baldwin, James. Go Tell It on the Mountain. N.Y., Knopf, 1953. 303p. *"The best of Baldwin's novels...and his best is very good indeed. It ranks...as a major contribution to American fiction." Bone. The Negro Novel in America.*

Baldwin, James. Going to Meet the Man. N.Y., Dial, 1965. 249p. *Short stories.*

Baldwin, James. Tell Me How Long the Train's Been Gone. N.Y., Dial, 1968. 484p.

Baldwin, James. This Morning, This Evening, So Soon. Frankfurt, Diesterweg, 1962. 60p. paper *Story later included in 'Going to Meet the Man.'*

Barrett, Nathan. Bars of Adamant; a Tropical Novel. N.Y., Fleet, 1966. 287p. *Set in Jamaica where the author has spent much of his life.*

Battles, Jesse Moore. Somebody Please Help Me. N.Y., Pageant, 1966 c1965. 116p.

Bellinger, Claudia. Wolf Kitty. N.Y., Vantage 1959. 173p.

Bennett, Hal. The Black Wine. N.Y., Doubleday 1968. 312p. *Novel about seven year-old David Hunter of Burnside, Va., who migrates to a New Jersey ghetto. "This fast paced novel ends as he approaches manhood. A violent coming of age, laced with rich Afro-American humor." Charles Wright. N.Y. Times Book Rev.*

Bennett, Hal. A Wilderness of Vines. N.Y., Doubleday, 1966. 345p. *The story of color discrimination among blacks in a rural Virginia community.*

Boles, Robert. Curling. Boston, Houghton, 1967. 259p.

Boles, Robert. The People One Knows. Boston, Houghton, 1964. 177p. *"Robert Boles is that rare writer on Negro life who sees the race problem as only one variation in a multitude of human problems." Cade Ware. Book Week.*

Bosworth, William. The Long Search. Great Barrington, Mass., Advance Pub. Co., 1957. 303p.

Branch, Edward. The High Places. N.Y., Exposition, 1957. 114p.

Brooks, Gwendolyn. Maud Martha. N.Y., Harper, 1953. 180p. *A sensitive series of sketches about the life of a young black girl growing up in Chicago, picturing her youth, marriage and motherhood as the moments she loved most.*

Brown, Frank London. Trumbull Park. Chicago, Regnery, 1959. 432p. *An effective story of the attempt of a small group of black families to move into a white housing project.*

Brown, Mattye Jeanette. The Reign of Terror. N.Y., Vantage, 1962. 119p.

Browne, Theodore. The Band Will Not Play Dixie; a Novel of Suspense. N.Y., Exposition, 1955. 151p.

Buster, Greene. Brighter Sun; an Historical Account of the Struggles of a Man to Free Himself and His Family from Human Bondage, by His Grandson. N.Y., Pageant, 1954. 282p.

Carrere, Mentis. Man in the Cane. N.Y., Vantage, 1956. 160p.

Chantrelle, Seginald. Not Without Dust. N.Y., Exposition, 1954. 123p.

Clinton, Dorothy Randle. The Maddening Scar, a Mystery Novel. Boston, Christopher, 1962. 117p.

Cook, Douglas. Choker's Son. N.Y., Comet, 1959. 31p.

Coolidge, Fay Liddle. Black Is White. N.Y., Vantage, 1958. 157p.

Cooper, Clarence L., Jr. Black! Two Short Novels. Evanston, Ill., Regency, 1963. 155p. paper *'Yet Princes Follow,' pp. 7-102; 'Not We Many,' pp. 103-155.*

Cooper, Clarence L., Jr. The Dark Messenger. Evanston, Ill., Regency, 1962. 157p. paper

Cooper, Clarence L., Jr. The Farm. N.Y., Crown, 1967. 248p. *Describes the experiences of a drug addict and peddler who is completing his sentence at a federal narcotics prison.*

Cooper, Clarence L., Jr. The Scene. N.Y., Crown, 1960. 310p. *Novel about heroin written while in prison.*

Cooper, Clarence L., Jr. Weed. Evanston, Ill., Regency, 1961. 159p. paper *Novel about marijuana.*

Cooper, John L. Opus One. N.Y., Maelstrom, 1966. 81p. paper

Cooper, William. Thank God for a Song; a Novel of Negro Church Life in the Rural South. N.Y., Exposition, 1962. 121p.

Corbo, D. R., Jr. Hard Ground. N.Y., Vantage 1954. 99p.

Correa, R. R. Rivera. *See Rivera Correa.*

Cotton, Ella Earls. Queen of Persia, the Story of Esther Who Saved Her People. Illus. by Stina Nagel. N.Y., Exposition, 1960. 150p.

Crump, George Peter, Jr. From Bondage They Came. N.Y., Vantage, 1954. 213p.

Crump, Paul. Burn, Killer, Burn. Chicago, Johnson, 1962. 391p. *Novel by a convicted murderer.*

Cunningham, George, Jr. Lily-Skin Lover, His Passion for Light-Complexioned Women Leads Him to Destruction. N.Y., Exposition, 1960 54p.

Davis, Charles. Two Weeks to Find a Killer. N.Y., Carlton, 1966. 77p. *Mystery.*

Davis, Joseph A. Black Bondage; a Novel of a Doomed Negro in Today's South. N.Y., Exposition, 1959. 175p.

Delany, Samuel R. Babel-17. N.Y., Ace, 1966. 173p. paper *Science fiction.*

Delany, Samuel R. The Ballad of Beta-2. Alpha Yes, Terra No, by Emil Petaja. N.Y., Ace, 1965. 96p. 156p. paper *Science fiction.*

Delany, Samuel R. Captives of the Flame. The Psionic Menace, by Keith Woodcott. N.Y., Ace, 1963. 147p. 108p. paper *Science fiction.*

Delany, Samuel R. City of a Thousand Suns. N.Y., Ace, 1965. 156p. paper *Science fiction.*

Delany, Samuel R. The Einstein Intersection. N.Y., Ace, 1967. 142p. paper *Science fiction.*

Delany, Samuel R. Empire Star. The Tree Lord of Imeton, by Tom Purdom. N.Y., Ace, 1966. 102p. 152p. paper *Science fiction.*

Delany, Samuel R. The Jewels of Aptor. Second Ending, by James White. N.Y., Ace, 1962. 156p. 100p. paper *Science fiction.*

Delany, Samuel R. The Jewels of Aptor. Rev. & enl. ed. N.Y., Ace, 1968. 159p. paper

Delany, Samuel R. Nova. N.Y., Doubleday, 1968. 279p. *Science fiction.*

Delany, Samuel R. The Towers of Toron. The Lunar Eye, by Robert M. Williams. N.Y., Ace, 1964. 140p. 115p. paper *Science fiction.*

Demby, William. The Catacombs. N.Y., Pantheon, 1965. 244p. *Novel about a black actress living in Rome.*

Diggs, Arthur. Black Woman. N.Y., Exposition, 1954. 43p.

Dreer, Herman. The Tie That Binds; a Novel of a Youth Who Seeks to Understand Life. Boston, Meador, 1958. 374p.

Du Bois, W. E. B. Mansart Builds a School. N.Y., Mainstream, 1959. 367p. (The Black Flame, Book Two) *Part of an autobiographical trilogy of novels by one of the great black leaders of this century.*

Du Bois, W. E. B. The Ordeal of Mansart. N.Y., Mainstream, 1957. 316p. (The Black Flame, Book One)

Du Bois, W. E. B. Worlds of Color. N.Y., Mainstream, 1961. 349p. (The Black Flame, Book Three)

Edwards, Junius. If We Must Die. N.Y., Doubleday, 1963. 137p. *Story of the attempt of a black veteran to register to vote in Mississippi.*

Edwards, S. W. Go Now in Darkness. Chicago, Baker Press, 1964. 255p.

English, Rubynn M. Citizen U. S. A. N.Y., Pageant, 1957. 318p.

Fair, Ronald L. Hog Butcher. N.Y., Harcourt, 1966. 182p.

Fair, Ronald L. Many Thousand Gone; an American Fable. N.Y., Harcourt, 1965. 114p. *A fable which imagines a county in Mississippi where slavery has been preserved.*

Farrell, John T. The Naked Truth. N.Y., Vantage, 1961. 196p.

Felton, James A. Fruits of Enduring Faith; a Story of Racial Unity. N.Y., Exposition, 1965. 96p.

Fenderson, Harold. The Phony and Other Stories. N.Y., Exposition, 1959. 139p.

Ferguson, Ira Lunan. The Biography of G. Wash Carter, White; Life Story of a Mississippi Peckerwood Whose Short Circuit Logic Kept Him Fantastically Embroiled. San Francisco, Lunan-Ferguson, 1969. 253p. *Jamaica-born author.*

Ferguson, Ira L. Ocee McRae, Texas; a Novel of Passion, Petroleum and Politics in the Pecos River Valley. N.Y., Exposition, 1962. 182p.

Ferguson, Ira Lunan. Which One of You Is Interracial? A Novelette and Other Stories. San Francisco, Lunan-Ferguson, 1969. 134p.

Fisher, William. The Waiters. Cleveland, World, 1953. 295p.

Flemister, John T. Furlough from Hell, a Fantasy. N.Y., Exposition, 1964. 103p.

Forster, Christine, pseud. (Christine Forte). A View from the Hill. N.Y., Vantage, 1964. 100p. *Author born in the West Indies.*

Gaines, Ernest J. Bloodline. N.Y., Dial, 1968. 249p. *Short stories.*

Gaines, Ernest J. Catherine Carmier. N.Y., Atheneum, 1964. 248p. *A commendable first novel by a native Louisianian. It tells of a young man's return to his rural hometown community in Louisiana.*

Gaines, Ernest J. Of Love and Dust. N.Y., Dial, 1967. 281p. *"...has succeeded where many others of his race have failed: he has written a book about Negroes and whites as just plain people, sharing equally the blame for maintaining a worn out tradition." James Lea. Sat. Rev.*

Gibson, Richard. A Mirror for Magistrates. London, A. Blond, 1958. 172p.

Greenlee, Sam. The Spook Who Sat By the Door. London, Allison & Busby, 1969. 182p. *Novel about a black CIA double agent.*

Groves, John Wesley. Pyrrhic Victory, a Collection of Short Stories. Philadelphia, United, 1953. 60p.

Gunn, Bill. All the Rest Have Died. N.Y., Delacorte, 1964. 220p.

Guy, Rosa. Bird at My Window. Philadelphia, Lippincott, 1966 c1965. 282p. *Author born in Trinidad.*

Harris, Leon R. Run Zebra, Run! A Story of American Race Conflict. N.Y., Exposition, 1959. 260p.

Heard, Nathan C. Howard Street. N.Y., Dial, 1968. 284p. *A novel by an ex-convict about the black criminal class which exists in Newark's Third Ward.*

Hercules, Frank. I Want a Black Doll. N.Y., Simon & Schuster, 1967. 319p. *Novel about interracial marriage in the U.S., by a Trinidadian.*

Hercules, Frank. Where the Hummingbird Flies. N.Y., Harcourt, 1961. 212p. *Set in Trinidad.*

Hill, Roy L. Two Ways and Other Stories. State College, Pa., Commercial Printing, 1959. 44p.

Himes, Chester. Une Affaire de Viol, Roman. Traduit de l'Americain par Andre Mathieu. Postface de Christiane Rochefort. Paris, Editions les Yeux Ouverts, 1963. 171p. paper *Not yet published in English. A novel about the alleged rape of a white woman by four black men. Set in Paris.*

Himes, Chester. All Shot Up. N.Y., Avon, 1960. 160p. paper *A Coffin Ed Johnson - Grave Digger Jones mystery.*

Himes, Chester. The Big Gold Dream. N.Y., Avon, 1960. 160p. paper *A Coffin Ed Johnson - Grave Digger Jones mystery.*

Himes, Chester. Blind Man With a Pistol. N.Y., Morrow, 1969. 240p. *A Coffin Ed Johnson - Grave Digger Jones mystery.*

Himes, Chester. Cotton Comes to Harlem. N.Y., Putnam, 1965. 223p. *A Coffin Ed Johnson - Grave Digger Jones mystery.*

Himes, Chester. The Crazy Kill. N.Y., Avon, 1959. 160p. paper *A Coffin Ed Johnson - Grave Digger Jones mystery.*

Himes, Chester. For Love of Imabelle. Greenwich, Conn., Fawcett, 1957. 157p. *A longer version appeared as A Rage in Harlem. N.Y., Avon, 1965. 192p.* paper *Jean Cocteau called this work "a prodigious masterpiece."*

Himes, Chester. The Heat's On. N.Y., Putnam, 1966. 220p. *A Coffin Ed Johnson - Grave Digger Jones mystery.*

Himes, Chester. Pinktoes. Paris, Olympia, 1961. 207p. paper Later published: N.Y., Putnam, 1965. 256p.

Himes, Chester. The Primitive. N.Y., New American Library, 1956 c1955. 151p. paper

Himes, Chester. The Real Cool Killers. N.Y., Avon, 1959. 160p. paper *A Coffin Ed Johnson - Grave Digger Jones mystery.*

Himes, Chester. Run Man Run. N.Y., Putnam, 1966. 192p. *Mystery.*

Himes, Chester. The Third Generation. Cleveland, World, 1954. 350p. *"In spite of its excesses, it has within it elements of great interest and it again demonstrates that Mr. Himes' talents are of a high order." Martin Levin. Sat. Rev.*

Hodges, George W. Swamp Angel. N.Y., New Voices, 1958. 128p.

Hooks, Nathaniel. Town on Trial; a Novel of Racial Violence in a Southern Town. N.Y., Exposition, 1959. 165p.

Horsman, Gallan. The Noose and the Spear; a Tale of Passion, Adventure and Violence. N.Y., Vantage, 1965. 88p.

Hough, Florenz H. Black Paradise. Philadelphia, Dorrance, 1953. 236p.

Hughes, Langston. The Best of Simple. N.Y., Hill & Wang, 1961. 245p.

Hughes, Langston. Simple Stakes a Claim. N.Y., Rinehart, 1957. 191p. *"This, the best of the 'Simples' so far, is a delight to read, essentially a spoof of racial questions plaguing America..." M. S. Byam. Library Journal.*

Hughes, Langston. Simple Takes a Wife. N.Y., Simon & Schuster, 1953. 240p. *Stories of black life in Harlem told through conversations between the author and Mr. Jesse B. Semple (better Known as Simple).*

Hughes, Langston. Simple's Uncle Sam. N.Y., Hill & Wang, 1965. 180p.

Hughes, Langston. Something in Common and Other Stories. N.Y., Hill & Wang, 1963. 236p.

Hughes, Langston. Tambourines to Glory. N.Y., John Day, 1958. 188p. *A novel about two Harlem women who decide to start a church of their own. "More and more the writing of Hughes tends to become an affair of the heart with Harlem. 'Tambourines to Glory' is funny as all get out, but it's no joke." Arna Bontemps. N.Y. Herald Tribune Bk. Rev.*

Humphrey, Lillie Muse. Aggie. N.Y., Vantage, 1955. 112p.

Hunter, Helen. Magnificent White Men. N.Y., Vantage, 1964. 153p. *Science fiction.*

Hunter, Kristin. God Bless the Child. N.Y., Scribner, 1964. 307p. *A promising first novel which concerns the obsession of a black girl for money and luxuries and examines the affect of ghetto life on its heroine.*

Hunter, Kristin. The Landlord. N.Y., Scribner, 1966. 338p. *A rather witty look at a white landlord and his black tenants. The location is in an unnamed Northern city.*

Jackson, W. Warner. The Birth of the Martyr's Ghost. N.Y., Comet, 1957. 167p.

James, Beauregard, pseud. The Road to Birmingham. N.Y., Bridgehead, 1964. 191p.

Johnson, Evelyn Allen. My Neighbor's Island. N.Y., Exposition, 1965. 55p.

Johnson, William M. The House on Corbett Street; a Novel of Negro Stirrings Amid Discontent. N.Y., William-Frederick, 1967. 311p.

Jones, LeRoi. The System of Dante's Hell. N.Y., Grove, 1965. 154p. *An account of childhood and adolescence in the black slums of Newark, the experiences of a Northern black in a small Southern town and glimpses of life in New York City.*

Jones, LeRoi. Tales. N.Y., Grove, 1967. 132p. *Short stories.*

Jones, Ralph H. The Pepperpot Man. N.Y., Vantage, 1965. 197p.

Jones, William H. The Triangle's End. N.Y., Exposition, 1954. 79p.

Jordan, Elsie. Strange Sinner. N.Y., Pageant, 1954. 172p.

Kelley, William Melvin. Dancers on the Shore. N.Y., Doubleday, 1964. 201p. *Sixteen short stories.*

Kelley, William Melvin. Dem. N.Y., Doubleday, 1967. 210p. *Satire on whites.*

Kelley, William Melvin. A Different Drummer. N.Y., Doubleday, 1962. 223p. *A well-written first novel that revolves about the decision of all of the blacks in a Southern state to move out, en masse.*

Kelley, William Melvin. A Drop of Patience. N.Y., Doubleday, 1965. 237p. *Novel about a blind black jazz musician.*

Kennedy, Mark. The Pecking Order. N.Y., Appleton, 1953. 278p. *"...has caught the language and meanings of Negro youngsters like no other book I have ever read." Roi Ottley. Chicago Sunday Tribune.*

Killens, John Oliver. And Then We Heard the Thunder. N.Y., Knopf, 1963 c1962. 485p. *A powerful novel of black soldiers in World War II.*

Killens, John Oliver. 'Sippi. N.Y., Trident, 1967. 434p.

Killens, John Oliver. Slaves. N.Y., Pyramid, 1969. 142p. paper

Killens, John Oliver. Youngblood. N.Y., Dial, 1954. 566p. *Story of a family of Georgia blacks during the early years of the 20th century. "This is a fine novel, vivid, readable, even its minor characters ...are as arresting as its major ones." Ann Petry. N.Y. Herald Tribune.*

Kirk, Paul. No Need to Cry. N.Y., Carlton, 1967. 215p.

LaHon, Vyola Therese. The Big Lie. N.Y., Vantage, 1964. 68p.

Lee, Audrey. The Clarion People. N.Y., McGraw, 1968. 180p. *Ghetto life as seen through the eyes of a black girl who leaves the country for the big city, presumably Philadelphia, where she gets a hospital job.*

Lee, Audrey. The Workers. N.Y., McGraw, 1969. 180p.

Lee, James F. The Victims. N.Y., Vantage, 1959. 190p.

Lipscomb, Ken. Duke Casanova. N.Y., Exposition, 1958. 76p.

Lucas, Curtis. Angel. N.Y., Lion, 1953. 160p. paper

Lucas, Curtis. Forbidden Fruit. N.Y., Universal, 1953. 135p. paper

Lucas, Curtis. Lila. N.Y., Lion, 1955. 190p. paper

McPherson, James Alan. Hue and Cry; Short Stories. Boston, Little, 1969. 275p.

Madden, Will Anthony. Five More; Short Stories. N.Y., Exposition, 1963. 64p.

Madden, Will Anthony. Two and One; 2 Short Stories and a Play. N.Y., Exposition, 1961. 50p.

Mahoney, William. Black Jacob. N.Y., Macmillan, 1969. 247p. *About a black Mississippi physician who has decided to run for Congress. The author has been an active SNCC field worker for the past decade.*

Major, Clarence. All-Night Visitors. N.Y., Olympia, 1969. 203p. *Pornographic.*

Marshall, Paule. Brown Girl, Brownstones. N.Y., Random House, 1959. 310p. *A first novel about black immigrants from Barbados who move into a 'brownstone' in Brooklyn, and who must therefore adjust to the subtleties of racial differentiation in the U. S.*

Marshall, Paule. The Chosen Place, the Timeless People. N.Y., Harcourt, 1969. 472p.

Marshall, Paule. Soul Clap Hands and Sing. N.Y., Atheneum, 1961. 177p. *Four short stories. "Not only is the language poetic, endowed with a freshness and beauty seldom encountered in modern fiction, but there also is a structural unity within each story..." Nick Aaron Ford. Phylon.*

Mayfield, Julian. The Grand Parade. N.Y., Vanguard, 1961. 448p. *A novel dealing with the school segregation crisis.*

Mayfield, Julian. The Hit. N.Y., Vanguard, 1957. 212p. *"As a fictional exploration into a comparatively new field of subject matter - the numbers game - 'The Hit' is a first novel of unusual interest..." Langston Hughes. N.Y. Herald Tribune Book Review.*

Mayfield, Julian. The Long Night. N.Y., Vanguard, 1958. 156p.

Mays, Willie and Jeff Harris. Danger in Center Field. Larchmont, N. Y., Argonaut, 1963. 192p. *Baseball mystery.*

Moreau, Julian, pseud. (J. Denis Jackson). The Black Commandos. Atlanta, Cultural Intitute Press, 1967. 228p. *Novel about the takeover of the U. S. by blacks.*

Montague, W. Reginald. Ole Man Mose; a Novel of the Tennessee Valley. N.Y., Exposition, 1957. 121p.

Morrison, C. T. The Flame in the Icebox; an Episode of the Vietnam War. N.Y., Exposition, 1968. 112p.

Motley, Willard. Let No Man Write My Epitaph. N.Y., Random House, 1958. 467p.

Motley, Willard. Let Noon Be Fair. N.Y., Putnam, 1966. 416p. *Set in Mexico.*

Offord, Carl. The Naked Fear. N.Y., Ace, 1954. 160p. paper *Trinidad-born author.*

Ottley, Roi. White Marble Lady. N.Y., Farrar, 1965. 278p.

Parks, Gordon. The Learning Tree. N.Y., Harper, 1963. 303p. *Novel about a black child growing up in a small Kansas town.*

Parrish, Clarence R. Images of Democracy (I Can't Go Home). N.Y., Carlton, 1967. 161p.

Paulding, James E. Sometime Tomorrow. N.Y., Carlton, 1965. 138p.

Peebles, Melvin van. A Bear for the FBI. N.Y., Trident, 1968. 157p.

Peebles, Melvin van. Le Chinois du XIVe. Paris, Martineau, 1966. 173p. paper *Stories, written in French.*

Perry, Charles. Portrait of a Young Man Drowning. N.Y., Simon & Schuster, 1962. 307p.

Petry, Ann. The Narrows. Boston, Houghton, 1953. 428p. *"...Ann Petry has achieved something as rare as it is commendable. Her book reads like a New England novel, and an unusually gripping one." Arna Bontemps. Sat. Rev.*

Pharr, Robert Deane. The Book of Numbers. N.Y., Doubleday, 1969. 374p. *This first novel is set in a Southern city in the 1930's. "The writer's creation of the black ward is a real accomplishment, and the vitality in the social structure of a community is beautifully presented." Martin Levin. N.Y. Times Book Rev.*

Phillips, Jane. Mojo Hand. N.Y., Trident, 1966. 180p.

Polite, Carlene Hatcher. The Flagellants. N.Y., Farrar, 1967. 214p. First published in Paris in a French translation. *"...Miss Polite's novel is a marker at the start of a new period in Negro fiction:... fiction in which conventional political action...has declined in relevance..." Stanley Kauffmann. New Republic*

Pollard, Freeman. Seeds of Turmoil; a Novel of American PW's Brainwashed in Korea. N.Y., Exposition, 1959. 264p.

Potter, Valaida. Sunrise Over Alabama. N.Y., Comet, 1959. 70p.

Pretto, Clarita C. The Life of Autumn Holliday. N.Y., Exposition, 1958. 95p. *Author born in the Virgin Islands.*

Puckett, G. Henderson. One More Tomorrow. N.Y., Vantage, 1959. 288p.

Ramsey, Leroy L. The Trial and the Fire. N.Y., Exposition, 1967. 160p.

Reed, Ishmael. The Free-Lance Pallbearers. N.Y., Doubleday, 1967. 155p.

Reed, Ishmael. Yellow Back Radio Broke-Down. N.Y., Doubleday, 1969. 177p.

Rhodes, Hari. A Chosen Few. N.Y., Bantam, 1965. 248p. paper *Novel about black Marines.*

Rivera Correa, R. R. The Pariahs. N.Y., Carlton, 1967. 60p.

Roberson, Sadie L. Killer of the Dream; Short Stories. N.Y., Comet, 1963. 95p.

Robinson, J. Terry. White Horse in Harlem. N.Y., Pageant, 1965. 159p.

Robinson, Rose. Eagle in the Air. N.Y., Crown, 1969. 159p.

Rogers, Joel A. She Walks in Beauty. Los Angeles, Western Publishers, 1963. 316p. *Jamaica-born author.*

Rollins, Bryant. Danger Song. N.Y., Doubleday, 1967. 280p. *Set in the Roxbury section of Boston, this novel is about two families, one white and respected, the other Boston ghetto blacks who have been beaten down by the world.*

Rollins, Lamen. The Human Race a Gang. N.Y., Carlton, 1965. 85p.

Scott, Anne. Case 999; a Christmas Story. Boston, Meador, 1953. 27p.

Screen, Robert Martin. We Can't Run Away from Here. N.Y., Vantage, 1958. 55p.

Shaw, Letty M. Angel Mink. N.Y., Comet, 1957. 137p.

Shores, Minnie T. Americans in America. Boston, Christopher, 1966. 115p.

Shores, Minnie T. Publicans and Sinners. N.Y., Comet, 1960. 172p.

Simmons, Herbert. Corner Boy. Boston, Houghton, 1957. 266p. *"His style is bold and strong, his imagination fresh, his sense of drama sure, his feelings uncluttered." Saunders Redding. Sat. Rev.*

Simmons, Herbert. Man Walking on Eggshells. Boston, Houghton, 1962. 250p. *Novel about a black ghetto-born jazz musician.*

Skinner, Theodosia B. Ice Cream from Heaven. N.Y., Vantage, 1962. 83p. *Short stories.*

Slim, Iceberg, pseud. (Robert Beck). Mama Black Widow. Los Angeles, Holloway House, 1969. 312p. paper

Slim, Iceberg, pseud. (Robert Beck). Pimp; the Story of My Life. Los Angeles, Holloway House, 1967. 317p. paper

Slim, Iceberg, pseud. (Robert Beck). Trick Baby; the Biography of a Con Man. Los Angeles, Holloway House, 1967. 312p. paper

Smith, Joe, pseud. Dagmar of Green Hills. N.Y., Pageant, 1957. 124p. *Science fiction.*

Smith, William Gardner. South Street. N.Y., Farrar, 1954. 312p.

Smith, William Gardner. The Stone Face. N.Y., Farrar, 1963. 213p. *Much of this story is set in Paris. "On the whole, this is the best...novel by a Negro writer since Ellison's 'Invisible Man.' Nick Aaron Ford. Phylon.*

Smythwick, Charles A., Jr. False Measure; a Satirical Novel of the Lives and Objectives of Upper Middle-Class Negroes. N.Y., William-Frederick, 1954. 285p.

Spence, Tomas H. and Eric Heath. Martin Larwin. N.Y., Pageant, 1954. 137p.

Sydnor, W. Leon. Veronica. N.Y., Exposition, 1956. 207p.

Talbot, Dave. The Musical Bride. N.Y., Vantage, 1962. 249p.

Tarter, Charles L. Family of Destiny. N.Y., Pageant, 1954. 277p.

Teague, Robert L. The Climate of Candor; a Novel of the 1970's. N.Y., Pageant, 1962. 198p.

Thomas, Will. The Seeking. N.Y., Wyn, 1953. 290p.

Turpin, Waters Edward. The Rootless. N.Y., Vantage, 1957. 340p.

Vanderpuije, Nii A. The Counterfeit Corpse. N.Y., Comet, 1956. 138p. *Mystery by a Liberian-born author.*

Van Dyke, Henry. Blood of Strawberries. N.Y., Farrar, 1968. 277p. *"...a highly literate and vastly entertaining suspense-comedy about some well-heeled Bohemians... sure-footed writing about the New York intellectual scene." Richard Freeman. Book World.*

Van Dyke, Henry. Ladies of the Rachmaninoff Eyes. N.Y., Farrar, 1965. 214p.

Vaught, Estella V. Vengeance is Mine. N.Y., Comet, 1959. 62p.

Vroman, Mary E. Esther. N.Y., Bantam, 1963. 154p. paper

Walker, Margaret. Jubilee. Boston, Houghton, 1966. 497p. *The story of a black woman who was born into slavery in Georgia during the early nineteenth century and lived through the Reconstruction period. This novel is based on the true life story of the author's great grandmother.*

Wallace, Elizabeth West. Scandal at Daybreak. N.Y., Pageant, 1954. 167p.

Wamble, Thelma. All in the Family. N.Y., New Voices, 1953. 199p.

Ward, Thomas Playfair. The Clutches of Circumstances. N.Y., Pageant, 1954. 164p.

Ward, Thomas Playfair. The Right to Live. N.Y., Pageant, 1953. 249p.

Ward, Thomas Playfair. The Truth That Makes Men Free. N.Y., Pageant, 1955. 154p.

Warner, Samuel J. Madam President-Elect. N.Y., Exposition, 1956. 249p.

Washington, Doris V. Yulan. N.Y., Carlton, 1964. 100p.

Watson, Lydia, pseud. (E. H. White). Our Homeward Way; a Novel of Race Relations in Modern Life. N.Y., Exposition, 1959. 163p.

Webb, Charles Lewis. Sasebo Diary. N.Y., Vantage, 1964. 129p.

Wells, Jack Calvert. Out of the Deep. Boston, Christopher, 1958. 369p.

Wells, Moses Peter. Three Adventurous Men. N.Y., Carlton, 1963. 55p.

West, John B. Bullets Are My Business. N.Y., New American Library, 1960. 128p. paper *Mystery*.

West, John B. Cobra Venom. N.Y., New American Library, 1960 c1959. 126p. paper *Mystery*.

West, John B. Death on the Rocks. N.Y., New American Library, 1961 c1960. 128p. paper *Mystery*.

West, John B. An Eye for an Eye. N.Y., New American Library, 1959. 144p. paper *Mystery*.

West, John B. Never Kill a Cop. N.Y., New American Library, 1961. 128p. paper *Mystery*.

West, John B. A Taste for Blood. N.Y., New American Library, 1960. 140p. paper *Mystery*.

West, William. Cornered. N.Y., Carlton, 1964. 134p.

Whitney, Jim E. Wayward O'er Tuner Sheffard. N.Y., Carlton, 1968. 186p.

Wideman, John Edgar. A Glance Away. N.Y., Harcourt, 1967. 186p. *A novel which describes one day in the life of a young black narcotics addict.*

Wiggins, Walter, Jr. Dreams in Reality of the Undersea Craft. N.Y., Pageant, 1954. 206p.

Williams, Jerome Ardell. The Tin Box; a Story of Texas Cattle and Oil. N.Y., Vantage, 1958. 275p.

Williams, John A. The Angry Ones. N.Y., Ace, 1960. 192p. paper

Williams, John A. The Man Who Cried I Am. Boston, Little, 1967. 403p.

Williams, John A. Night Song. N.Y., Farrar, 1961. 219p. *A novel whose main character is a jazz musician; said to be based on the life of Charlie Parker.*

Williams, John A. Sissie. N.Y., Farrar, 1963. 277p. *"...it is Sissie who looms largest. She may well be the authoritative portrait of the Negro mother in America...who has given the beleaguered Negro family whatever strength and stability it has." David Boroff. Sat. Rev.*

Williams, John A. Sons of Darkness, Sons of Light; a Novel of Some Probability. Boston, Little, 1969. 279p. *A thriller with much to say about our racial dilemma.*

Wilson, Carl T. D. The Half Caste. Ilfracombe, Stockwell, ca. 1962. 207p. *Set in London.*

Wilson, Pat. The Sign of Keloa. N.Y., Carlton, 1961. 36p.

Wooby, Philip. Nude to the Meaning of Tomorrow; a Novel of a Lonely Search. N.Y., Exposition, 1959. 285p.

Woods, William B. Lancaster Triple Thousand; a Novel of Suspense. N.Y., Exposition, 1956. 77p.

Wright, Charles. The Messenger. N.Y., Farrar, 1963. 217p.

Wright, Charles. The Wig; a Mirror Image. N.Y., Farrar, 1966. 179p.

Wright, Richard. Eight Men. Cleveland, World, 1961. 250p. *Eight short stories.*

Wright, Richard. Lawd Today. N.Y., Walker, 1963. 189p. *Set in Chicago during the depression.*

Wright, Richard. The Long Dream. N.Y., Doubleday, 1958. 384p. *"Richard Wright... has written a surging, superb new book which closely examines the anatomy of Southern racial prejudice and reveals some awful truths." Roi Ottley. Chicago Sunday Tribune.*

Wright, Richard. The Outsider. N.Y., Harper, 1953. 405p. *A melodrama about a black Chicago post office worker who changes his name, comes to New York, becomes involved with Communists, murders and in the end is killed by a member of the Party.*

Wright, Richard. Savage Holiday. N.Y., Avon, 1954. 220p. paper

Wright, Sarah E. This Child's Gonna Live. N.Y., Delacorte, 1969. 276p. *The story focuses on a black mother in an eastern Maryland ghetto whose dream is to migrate North. "The canon of the American folk epic is enriched by this small masterpiece. Shane Stevens. N.Y. Times Book Rev.*

Yerby, Frank. Benton's Row. N.Y., Dial, 1954. 346p.

Yerby, Frank. Captain Rebel. N.Y., Dial, 1956. 343p.

Yerby, Frank. The Devil's Laughter. N.Y., Dial, 1953. 376p.

Yerby, Frank. Fairoaks. N.Y., Dial, 1957. 405p.

Yerby, Frank. The Garfield Honor. N.Y., Dial, 1961. 347p.

Yerby, Frank. Gillian. N.Y., Dial, 1960. 346p.

Yerby, Frank. Goat Song, a Novel of Ancient Greece. N.Y., Dial, 1967. 498p.

Yerby, Frank. Griffin's Way. N.Y., Dial, 1962. 345p.

Yerby, Frank. Jarrett's Jade. N.Y., Dial, 1959. 342p.

Yerby, Frank. Judas, My Brother; the Story of the Thirteenth Disciple; an Historical Novel. N.Y., Dial, 1968. 540p.

Yerby, Frank. An Odor of Sanctity; a Novel of Medieval Moorish Spain. N.Y., Dial, 1965. 563p.

Yerby, Frank. The Old Gods Laugh; a Modern Romance. N.Y., Dial, 1964. 312p.

Yerby, Frank. The Serpent and the Staff. N.Y., Dial, 1958. 377p.

Yerby, Frank. Speak Now; a Modern Novel. N.Y., Dial, 1969. 227p.

Yerby, Frank. The Treasure of Pleasant Valley. N.Y., Dial, 1955. 348p.